P R O D U C T I O N S

The Islaamic Meeting

How to Plan and Attend

By Naseeb Khan

Dawah Gear Productions, Inc

Published by Dawah Gear Productions, Inc.

http://www.dawahgear.com

The Islaamic Meeting, How to Plan and Attend

Copyright by Naseeb Khan

© 2008 Dawah Gear Productions, Inc.

ISBN: 978-0-615-22377-3

Whoever looks forward [with hope and awe] to **meeting** Allah [on Resurrection Day, let him be ready for it]: for, behold, the end set by Allah [for everyone's life] is bound to come—and He alone is all-hearing, all-knowing!

(Al-Qur'aan Chapter 29 Verse 5)

A Brief Word

This book captures my experience with meetings over the many years of working with Muslims in various organizations and groups. I have tried my best to present this typically boring and academic subject in as lighthearted a manner as possible. My goal is to provide a reference which young people can use to learn about this important skill.

I dedicate this book to all the Islaamic Workers who spend so much time in meetings. I also dedicate this book to my various teachers who sacrificed their time in order to teach me how to be a better person and human being. May Allah protect them always, forgive their sins and reward them with Jannah (Paradise). Ameen.

Gratitude

I want to thank Allah for allowing me the privilege of attending one of the greatest meetings of my life— the first meeting with my dear wife and best friend— Fazila. She continues daily to inspire and motivate me.

I also want to thank my parents, Najib and Amena, who have always supported me in all my endeavors even when it seemed crazy to them. I want to express how blessed I am to have two wonderful sisters, Haseena and Zameena whose unconditional love and support have never wavered.

I also thank Allah for the gift of having four wonderful children, Nabeeha, Raa'id, Wardah, and Jawaad; my son-in-law Naeem and my first grandson Yusuf. They continue to amaze me in so many wonderful ways. Finally, I remind myself that all good is from Allah and all mistakes in this book are from me. I seek Allah's forgiveness and mercy.

Naseeb Khan

Contents

1

So You Took a Chance

___

Congratulations!

You have decided to pick up a book about meetings. I am impressed. This means that either you are one of those nerdy types who get some kind of sadistic pleasure from reading books such as this one or that you are frustrated with so many, many meetings in your life and really want to do something about it. Of course it could be an entirely different reason altogether such as you are stranded on a lonely island and this is the only book that was rescued from the sinking ship (it could happen). Whatever the reason let me assure you that you have actually chosen the right book to read. It is true that meetings are one of those things which if not handled properly can really make you angry, frustrated, and sad. You come away from a useless meeting with a bad taste in your mouth. You want those hours back.

___

You feel as though you just returned from some strange encounter with people who had no appreciation or respect for you as a person or even cared for your opinions. It seemed as though you were at the meeting just to sit, be seen and not heard.

I know exactly how you feel as I have been attending meetings all my life. After a while I became so disgusted with this experience that I told myself I will champion the cause to rid the world of mediocre meetings and try to show everyone how to do it well. Of course this is plan B. Plan A was to rid the world of meetings altogether. I however realized that the problem was not the actual meeting but rather the people who organized them. Meetings when done well are actually great tools that lead to successful implementation of plans and projects.

Well, enough said. Let's get to it! After all, the reason you are reading this book is to find answers to the many questions on your mind. How can I make the meetings more useful? Should I attend or refuse? How can I find a way to get my opinions across? How do I get along with the loud mouthed obnoxious bullies who seem to frequent all of the meetings? You ponder these issues and wonder if there is a better way? Of course there is. Hopefully by the end of this book, you will have some answers to these and other such questions.

I want to assure you that by the end of this book, instead of hating meetings, you will actually look forward to them. They will become your classroom where you get to teach others how to do it well. You will rid yourself of the dreaded "anti-meeting syndrome" that we all share. You see, when we do not know why we hate something, we call it a syndrome. Let us make a pact between us that after you are finished with this book, you will try very hard to improve the meetings that are being held by Muslims and their groups.

To Do

1. Meetings Book
2. Youth Matters
3. Operations Handbook

Plan A

Rid the world of meetings!!

Plan B

The Islaamic Meeting

Plan C

??????????????

Meetings Attended this month...

~~||||~~ ~~||||~~
~~||||~~ ~~||||~~
~~||||~~ ~~||||~~
~~||||~~
|||

2

The Invitation

You get up in the morning and thanked the Lord for allowing you to be alive for another day. You tell yourself you are going to have a wonderful day. You even woke up for the Fajr Salaah and that was something that always leaves a good taste in your well brushed and cleansed mouth. You are ready. Your wonderful breakfast is already well settled in your stomach. You are now prepared to take on the world. You arrive at your workplace (or home office if you work from home). Then out of nowhere the sudden news arrives. It can come in the form of a phone call. It can come in the form of an email. It can even come in the form of a snail mail. (Snail mail? Yes this is the trendy name for regular mail delivered by the post office. I personally find the term offensive to these dedicated people).

Whatever way it came to you, the result is the same. You read or hear the chilling words "inviting you to a meeting". You pause for a moment to let your brain get over the initial shock. If you got it by email, you stare and reread the message with the hope that you had read it wrong. No such blessing. It is true. You are a chosen one. You have been selected from among the millions to attend a special meeting. I have never heard of any meeting not being special. You then start to think and think. How important is this meeting to me? What will be the consequences if I do not attend? What are the benefits to me? Can I really spare the time? Will there be anyone there who I do not like? Will this meeting result in more work for me? (What? Are you kidding me? You know the answer to this one. I have never attended any meeting that didn't result in more work for me).

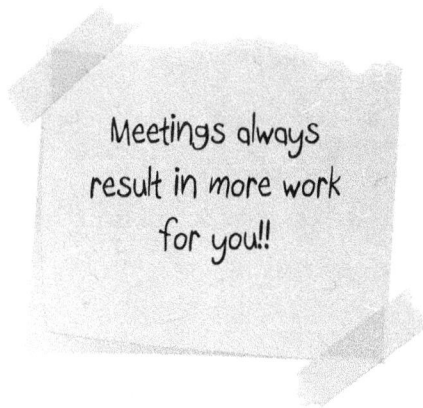

Meetings always
result in more work
for you!!

These and many such questions zip through the grey cells in your brain. Your day has now been truly spoilt. You now have to first check your calendar to see if you are available for the date. You have to reply to the invitation, one way or another. You then have to see if there are any preparations you have to make for the meeting. My goodness! You have not even agreed to the meeting as yet and already it has increased your workload. You know that as a Muslim, it is recommended that you accept invitations unless there are valid reasons for not doing so. You start to search your mind for excuses not to attend.

You think briefly about whether you can lie but quickly realize that this is not an option for Muslims. We are not allowed to lie. With no legitimate reason for not attending you quickly consider other alternatives. Ask the person who invited you whether you need to be physically present or not. Can you send your input via email or some other manner? If they say you must come in person, then don't give up. Depending on the type of meeting, ask them if you can come just for the part of the meeting that is relevant to you.

> Always ask if it is compulsory for you to attend the meeting

Sometimes you may be able to get out of the meeting with these tactics but most of the time you will get the response "what is wrong with you" or "this is Islaamic work, brother/sister". They end their statements emphasizing that "you must be there" or "it is very important that you attend". Finally you sigh and come to the conclusion that you have to really attend.

Now if you got invited over the phone to a meeting, be very careful how to reply. My personal recommendation is not to agree at that moment. You will regret such an impulsive act. Believe me it will haunt you for many nights. The best response to the person inviting you is that you have to check your schedule. They might try to bully you and say that they will hold on the line, while you check. Don't allow yourself to give in to this pressure tactic. Say to them that it is not possible for you to check this now. Then before they jump in to speak, quickly tell them what time and date they need to call you back to confirm. Did you read what I just wrote here? I said tell them that they should get back to you. Not the other way around. Never ever say that you will get back to them as this will be another task that you have to put on your already overloaded schedule and if you do not call them back as agreed, it becomes a black mark against you. Let them get back to you.

Let me say that if you are a member of a committee or a regular participant in a group, then the above does not apply. A different set of rules apply. Your involvement in the committee means that you have already committed yourself to attend all the mandatory meetings. Thus, if someone from the committee calls you to let you know about a future meeting, try to confirm your attendance immediately if you can or promise to call them back.

Yes, I said you call them back. This is part of your commitment to the committee which falls under a special circumstance.

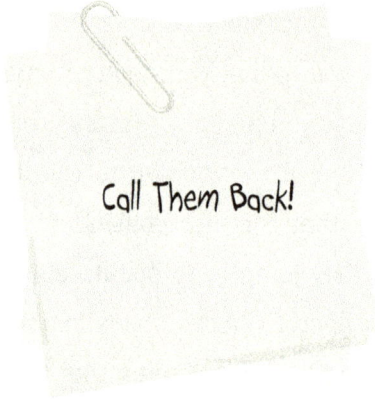

Call Them Back!

3

The Reply

After much thought you realize that you can't get out of the meeting. They want you there. You decide to attend the "special meeting". Now if you got the invitation by email, then reply as briefly and clearly as possible that you will accept the invitation to attend. If you got the invitation by a phone call, then you wait for them to call you back. As part of the reply there are some important things that must also be done. The first thing you want to do is have clear in your mind what kind of meeting it is and also what is to be your expected role. You should ensure that you receive an agenda for the meeting (we will get into what the agenda should have later). If the agenda is one of those poor, substandard, badly written productions, then, at a minimum, you need to find out the following: who else will be attending the meeting, where the meeting is being held, what time and date the meeting is scheduled for, and how long is the meeting expected to last. This should be enough for now. If the organizers insist that you cannot receive an agenda until you attend, then you may decide to opt out. In fact my personal preference is not to attend any meeting where the agenda has not been given to me prior to the meeting.

I am also aware that providing an agenda prior to a meeting may not always be practical. For example, in some poor countries where phones or emails are not available or it is too expensive or unreliable to post the agenda, it may not be possible to have the agenda sent to you. This is a rare exception. As a general rule, insist on being given the agenda prior to the meeting and get a contact number so that you can clarify any item on the agenda that may not make any sense to you.

Now, if you are not like me and feel that it is okay for you to attend the meeting without any agenda being given to you then I take my hat off to you. You are indeed a brave soul. At least, I would advise you to take a flask with your favorite beverage along with some snacks for yourself. Who knows when you will be leaving that meeting!

4

Attending the Meeting

The day has arrived and you have your tea in your flask, your notebook, fancy expensive pen, several types of delicious snacks, and you are off to the meeting. Already so much of your time has been invested in this one meeting. After all you had to make a special trip to the grocery store to get that herbal tea and those snacks you like so much. Nevertheless, you still feel a sense of pride as you tell yourself you are doing the work of Allah. You are trying to please Allah. You are doing your duty and being a good Muslim. You are actually glad you made the decision to come and now you look forward to contributing to the meeting. You arrive with five to ten minutes to spare and did not even get lost on the way or anything. You even found a good parking space. Wow.

It is a good sign and a mercy from Allah. You arrive at the actual meeting room and all the good feelings you had immediately disappears. You take one look around and realize that you have just been invited to a meeting that was not properly organized. You kick yourself for coming to a meeting where no agenda was given to you. That was a red flag and you ignored it anyway. You wanted to believe in your fellow Muslims. You wanted to trust them. You wanted to hope that they knew what they were doing. It is too late to back out now. You are here. Take a sip from the flask and smile.

It was not only the poorly lighted room that was the problem. You notice that only the Chairperson and two others have arrived at the meeting. They are sitting and waiting. You take a napkin from your bag, wipe your chair and sit down. You have now become a participant in the great waiting game. You are being punished for coming early. You poor fool.

They are actually sitting and waiting for the latecomers. These latecomers who have not yet arrived to the meeting are being given more priority than you. The meeting time is being pushed back to make it more convenient to those who come late. Your time counts for nothing. You sit and look at your cell phone to see the time. Five, ten, fifteen, thirty minutes go by. The meeting is still in waiting mode as members slowly trickle in and take their seats. Some apologize while others sit without a wink or pause of breath.

Finally, you cannot bear it anymore and gently inquire from the Chairperson when will the meeting begin. "Soon" was the reply. You feel foolish. Soon? What kind of answer is this? What did you get yourself into? After forty five minutes the meeting finally gets underway. You leave the meeting never wanting to return. You secretly tell yourself that if you did return you will be coming late. You know deep down that your Islaamic conscience will not allow you to really do this. (What a sad plight).

This situation is just one of the many, many things that can happen when meetings are not organized and planned properly. It is important to recognize the symptoms of a bad meeting so that you are able to fix them effectively. The first thing a doctor does when you visit him or her is to try to figure out what is wrong with you. They then try to figure out what caused it to happen. Finally they suggest to you a possible remedy. We have to now take on the role of a doctor. We have to become a "meetings doctor."

Over the next few chapters I am going to give you real life examples of what can go wrong in meetings. All of what I am about to tell you has happened to me in meetings over the years.

We will examine some of them in detail so that you can have a better understanding of what I mean. Please take careful note of these situations. You will see them all of your life as you begin to attend more and more meetings. I call them "meeting nightmares."

5

The Bored Members Meeting

It is the wish of most of us to become so important that we get invited to the "Board" Members meeting but the reality is that we end up in the "Bored" Members meeting. I have attended many meetings of this type. The typical signs are that the attendees to the meeting do not really want to be there. One reason may be that they are being forced to attend due to some job commitments or organizational mandate and they do not see the relevance of the meeting to them. They are convinced that they are wasting their time in the meeting. They usually come late to the meeting. You look at their faces and see the tinge of frustration and borderline anger as they take their seats. The most common way they show protest is to spend their time in the meeting just doodling on their cheap notepads.

Some of the finest art work has been produced from these doodling sessions. If you do not know what doodling is, I am sorry for you. (Just go ask someone). Other factors that may contribute to this attitude is a lack of a clear agenda, long meetings or a case of "meeting-itis" (a sickness brought on by attending too many meetings).

Official Doodle Folder

Do NOT peek or touch!!!

6

Mystery Agenda Meeting

Quite strangely, I have attended my share of meetings where the agenda is a mystery. We are either not given an agenda or we are given it at the meeting itself. This sorry state of affairs is really traumatic and is a sure sign that you are in a badly planned meeting. Also, quite often the agenda that is given to you is so poorly written that you don't even know what you are expected to contribute. The items on the agenda give you no clue as to what kind of discussion or decision you are expected to make. For example, the agenda lists "picnic" as an item to be discussed and you sit there and wonder to yourself what this means. Picnic? It's a nice word. It conjures up a time of fun and leisure with family, friends and food. Yes that is true. But what are we here to discuss or decide about it? This is the mystery. Are we discussing the venue for the picnic? Are we deciding if we should have one? Are we identifying some persons to organize it? What?

We have to sit and wait for the powerful Chairperson to decipher this code. Only in a meeting setting will we allow someone to get away with this kind of behavior. In other aspects of life we would never allow it to happen to us. For example if your friend invites you to go on a driving trip and when you ask where we are going, he says "picnic", you would not leave it at that. You would want to ask other questions such as:

- Where are we going?
- How long will we be there for?
- Who will be there?
- Do I have to walk with food?
- Who is going to drive?
- Who is paying for gas?

Of course we would want answers to these questions. Have you noticed the price of gas lately? These are relevant and important questions. They allow you to decide if you need to walk with your sun tan lotion or your running shoes.

If for a simple driving trip we have all these questions, then why do we give ourselves permission to go to meetings without clearly understanding the agenda? I hate being invited to such kinds of meetings. The mere fact that you are not given an agenda is a clear sign that this meeting has a high possibility of being either ineffectual or an absolute disaster. I know I ranted about this earlier and so I will not repeat it again here except to remind you about the flask and snacks if you decide to go. The reality is that a lack of a clear agenda speaks volumes about the professionalism of the organizers of the meeting. If they invite you to a meeting, they must have some reason for the meeting, you would think. The minimum they can do is put those reasons on paper in the form of an agenda and distribute it.

Failing to do so gives one the impression that they don't really know why they want to meet. So I say if the organizers of the meeting don't know why they want to meet, then why should I attend?

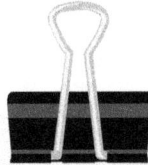

The reality is that a lack of a clear agenda speaks volumes about the professionalism of the organizers of the meeting.

7

Digression or Discussion

Whew! I cannot tell you how many times I have attended meetings where you sit with your pen and pad, your Wudu intact and ready for business only to realize that there are people in this meeting that can only be described as "special". These people are special because they are unaware that there is a world outside of theirs. They think that this world is only about them and their affairs alone. Thus you sit there and listen to their personal and irrelevant stories, anecdotes and useless talk. They talk and talk until your ears hurt to listen to their stories anymore. They are trying to make a point but the introduction to that point is so convoluted that they digress far from the topic at hand. The Chairperson being polite sits there and allows it to go on and on and ooooooooonnnnn.

You try very hard to send signals to the Chairperson. Your lip movements, head movements and eye twirling routine would get you hired in any bona fide circus but alas they are ignored by the Chairperson. You sit there and eventually are forced to reach into your snack pouch to get out your headache medication. You mentally send several memos to yourself. Note to self, never attend any meeting with this individual again.

You really want to reach across the table and GRAB this insensitive "special person" by the _____. *(You can fill in the blank space here. My treat to you, just keep it clean).*

You do nothing as you realize Islaam does not allow this behavior. You quietly resort to your last weapon which is to make dua' (prayer). The result of meetings with this scenario is that many hours are spent and very little is achieved by way of decisions.

8

Missing Data Meeting

The meetings that I detest the most are the ones where we do not have all the information at hand. I hate this kind of meeting because it is totally avoidable. I mean you come to the meeting and you have done your homework. You are ready to make decisions and move the goals forward. The meeting starts on time and everything seems to be going well when you hear the words "I guess we will have to reschedule this item for the next meeting." You ask why and then you are told by the Chairperson that "we do not have all the information we need to make the decision." Come on. Meetings are about data, schedules and assignments.

For example, the agenda says that we will be finalizing the venue for the picnic. Hasan checked the venue out and it is good and suitable for the event. As the members are just about to make a final decision, someone asks "How much does it cost?" There is an awkward silence as all eyes turn towards Hasan. He smiles sheepishly as he confesses that he did not find out that piece of information. The result is missing data! The decision is delayed.

Another example of this situation occurs when someone who has to do a task is absent for the meeting and did not let anyone know about the status of their assignment. Zaid was assigned at the last meeting to identify and confirm a guest speaker for the program. He was to report at the present meeting. He is absent. He did not let anyone know if his task was done or not. The decision is delayed because of missing data! We must not let our meetings be affected by this totally avoidable problem.

There must be someone who is responsible to ensure that all the data needed to make decisions are available. If not, then don't put it on the agenda. It is a sad commentary on the quality of the group or meeting when this happens. It leads to the wasting of each others time and shows disrespect for each other. Enough said.

9

Never Ending Meeting

Have you ever attended meetings where you are told to show up at 9 a.m. sharp for a meeting and you do so with great care and enthusiasm feeling proud of this fact? The meeting gets started and it is one of those meetings where they conveniently forgot to tell you when the meeting will end. You look at the agenda and realize that there is nothing there that gives you any clue as to when the meeting is expected to end. You glance around the room at the others to see if anyone else really cares. They are all comfortably engaged in animated discussions and no one seems to care about the passing time, only you! The Chairperson is allowing everyone to talk in detail about every topic and you sit there and become anxious.

Your fancy silver cell phone vibrates to inform you that you have to go to the mall for the twelve thirty sale. You need to be at that sale but you also want to be a dedicated worker. You realize that this meeting does not have an ending time or the ending has been pushed back due to the late comers. You really can't tell anyone you need to leave to go to the mall as they will think you are not a serious Islaamic worker. There goes your chance of having those new shoes.

How could you have been so silly to get caught attending an open ended meeting that did not have an ending time? This is totally unacceptable and you should never attend meetings without knowing the time of its ending. This messes up your busy schedule. At least if the meeting specifies an ending time and does not finish on time, you have a chance to say that you came with the expectation that it would be finished at the time indicated and you have to leave for another engagement.

10

Bullying For Attention

I know many of you can relate to this type of meeting. The ones where only one or two people are speaking continuously and you cannot get a word in edgewise. You politely wait for these people to pause or to catch a breath or at least to reach a full stop in their sentences, so that you can sneak in a word or two. Alas, no such chance. They just seem to speak as they breathe and you never get the opportunity to say anything. In desperation you decide to take a chance and say something just as they are finishing a sentence. You figure this is the best moment for you. They don't even slow down or stop and you find yourself talking at the same time as they are. These bullies instead of giving you a chance to make your point just continue to talk non-stop. On top of that they are also now looking at you and you can see their eyes (not mouths) saying to you "how dare you".

You begin to feel uncomfortable and politely stop talking in mid-sentence. You give this a couple of other tries but always end up with the same result. You keep quiet and become angry in silence.

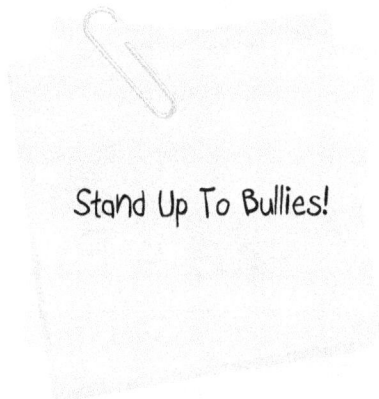

Stand Up To Bullies!

The Chairperson seems unable to control the discussion or is unaware of the situation. These "talking heads" seem to have several opinions on any and every topic on the floor and you sit there angry but unable to really participate.

Finally, you decide on another tactic. You raise your hand indicating that you want to say something. They either ignore you or say this is not kindergarten. They tell you if you have something to say, just say it. You embarrassingly take your hand down feeling foolish. This unfortunate situation should never be allowed to occur. You leave the meeting without being able to make a significant contribution. You are angry at both the Chairperson and all those bullies.

11

Let Us Take A Breather

You may be wondering why I am telling you about all these nightmares. I am conditioning you to develop an acute sense of awareness about them. I am arming you with the information so that you can be prepared. I am helping you to read the signs so that when you go to your next meeting you will have a different experience. You will be able to zone in on all of these signs easily. Later we will teach you how to deal with them. For now I have some more nightmares to share. We need to get them all out in the open. After all, you are the doctor and you need to find out all the symptoms that the patient has before we can prescribe suitable and comprehensive remedies, so hang in there.

Once we are through these stories, the good stuff will follow. This book will teach you the skills that you need to deal with all of these situations. In fact, by the end of this book, you will secretly crave to attend a meeting with these problems so that you can practice your new found skills. For now here are some more nightmares that you may see in your meetings.

12

Decisions or Pious Wishes

What a disaster this is! You attend the meeting and after many hours of discussing, arguing, listening to the life stories of several lonely souls who crave for attention, or fighting off the meeting bullies, we finally arrive at the all important decision making time. This is the "feel good" time for the meeting as we are about to make decisions and accomplish great things.

Everyone is happy. Even you are a little bit excited. Then suddenly it happens. The expected decisions do not come. Instead, we get what can only be categorized as pious wishes. For example, we decide that Davie Park is where we will have the picnic. This at first glance appears to be a good decision as the park is wonderful and has all the facilities needed for our picnic.

The problem is that a person to book the park was not identified nor was a deadline set by which the booking was to be made. No one is responsible.

The decision stands alone by itself and we get into the ridiculous problem of "everybody thought somebody would do it and so nobody did it." Thus these kinds of decisions just float around and become nothing more than pious wishes that will return to haunt you at the next meeting when it is not accomplished. To be a good decision all factors must be addressed so that the decision can easily be executed. At a minimum, the decision should be clearly worded, include a specific deadline and be assigned to some person or team.

13

Tedious Minutes

We gather people together, we discuss important matters, and we spend hours and make critical decisions. We now need to document this great meeting. The technical term "minutes" is what is used to call the document that records the crucial information about the meeting. The term "minutes" actually sends a signal that meetings should not be long tedious affairs.

The minutes of the meeting should not be essays which give a blow by blow narration of every point by every person that spoke at the meeting. The minutes are really just a proper recording of the key decisions and suggestions which should be written in a concise manner that facilitates action (more about this later).

When the minutes of the meetings are not well written, we get this muddled account that does not clearly identify the decisions and may even leave some of them out. This leads to misunderstandings of what is expected by the attendees regarding what and how to execute the decisions. When they fail to deliver as per expectations, it can lead to the nasty exercise of blame and name calling.

14

The Hot Chair

I have attended many meetings that were conducted by those who should not even be in such a meeting. This leads to frustrations and dismay. It's not by coincidence we call the person conducting the meeting "The Chairperson." The success of the meeting really rests with the Chairperson. They have to make sure all the preparatory work is done prior to the meeting. When the Chairperson is weak or unprepared or worse, untrained, we end up leaving the meeting with a bitter taste in our mouths. We feel as if we were abused and that we accomplished nothing much.

Untrained Chairpersons will falter at every step of the meeting. An untrained Chairperson will allow discussions to be irrelevant; they allow bullies to dominate the meeting; they are indecisive and take a long time to make decisions; they show bad time management skills; they are rude and obnoxious to the attendees of the meeting; and they don't allow everyone a chance to participate in the meeting. A bad Chairperson will constantly interject their opinion on every matter and try to get everyone to accept it. A bad Chairperson is a nightmare that must not be allowed to happen as it leads to the most traumatic type of meetings. Such meetings leave everyone attending with a sense of hopelessness. Nothing chases away people like a bad Chairperson.

15

Venue Victims

I hope you never get to attend one of these types of meetings where you go and get jammed into a small room so tight that you can smell the laundry detergent from each others clothes. The light is bad and the chair you are sitting in is really not a chair at all, it just resembles one. It slowly dawns on you that you are the victim of a bad venue selection.

Believe me; I have seen my fair share of terrible venues over the years. When the venue is not good, all kinds of problems can occur. I remember attending meetings in bad and unsafe neighborhoods. You are in the meeting but your thoughts are with your car parked outside. You are hoping you will see it again intact and safe. Such thoughts can make it difficult to concentrate on the meeting itself. The venue is certainly one of the factors that contribute to a successful meeting. It should be given due attention when planning the meeting.

16

Let Us Take Another Breather

That's it for now. These are some of the nightmare scenarios that can occur when meetings are not properly planned and executed. All of the previously mentioned meetings can be easily avoided and should never be allowed to happen. I am glad that you have decided to join me in my efforts to rid the world of bad meetings. Yes, I mean you! Why else are you still reading this book? Let me break it down for you. At the moment let's say you are in a meeting and we are conversing, at least I am. You are mulling over what I say and then you will decide what makes sense and hopefully you will act upon it. Why should we let so many people suffer through all those terrible meetings?

Join me and let us teach them how to do it better. We can even teach them how to do it bigger. If you are not on board as yet then that's fine too. Just keep reading. You may still change your mind along the way. However, before we move on, let us recap those symptoms of bad meetings one last time. They are as follows:

- Late Start

- Bored Members

- Mystery Agenda

- Digression Or Discussion

- Missing Data

- Never Ending

- Bullies

- Decisions Or Pious Wishes

- Tedious Minutes

- Bad Chairperson

- Poor Venue

17

Meetings Are Important

Meetings are vital and important for the success of any group or project. Here are some wonderful things to note about meetings and what makes them so special and relevant even today.

- It is a forum where human minds can interact and share ideas and thoughts to arrive at the best possible way forward.

- It is a place for people to align their perspectives to arrive at an agreed upon way of solving a problem.

- It is an opportunity to distribute and share tasks so that they can be completed easily.

- It is a format where decisions are made and acted upon.

- It is the space where new and wonderful suggestions are sought and noted.

- It is a forum where lifelong friendships are built, relationships are formed and networking opportunities emerge.

- It is a setting where we can get a chance to organize and become organized.

- Meetings force us to think and plan effectively.

- Meetings allow us to analyze and study situations with the hope of making them better.

- Meetings are the lifeblood of any group and when done well become the single most effective forum for change and progress.

This is important!
When can we meet?

You see, I told you I wasn't against meetings. They do have a very important place and purpose. We must try hard to make sure they serve that purpose. They are here to stay and will never go away as they are too critical. Therefore we should become better at dealing with them. Let me remind you that in the Qur'aan, Allah tells us that one of the hopes of the believers will be to meet Allah.

You see, even after we leave this world, we will still be involved in meetings. That one, by the way, will be the most important one of our lives. We must all prepare properly for it.

18

The Fundamental Elements

Now that we have understood what we must not do, let us take a look at what we must do. The first thing we must understand is what are the fundamental elements of this peculiar thing we call a "meeting." These are as follows:

- Meeting Organizer

- Venue

- Agenda

- Chairperson

- Attendees

- Minutes

- Protocols

Each of these items must be adequately catered for if the meeting is to be successful. We need to examine each of these in detail. It is not important which order we discuss these as they are all very important and critical. As you become more involved in Islaamic Activities, you may be called upon to take on different roles. You may have to be the meeting organizer for a meeting. Or you may be called upon to be the Chairperson. Certainly you will be an attendee and may even be asked to prepare the agenda or minutes. Thus we need to learn about each of these critical items.

19

The Meeting Organizer

The Meeting Organizer is the one who is responsible for planning the meeting. Before I continue, let me pause and talk to my fellow Islaamic Workers for a moment. A meeting is a forum where we are asking serious Muslims to spend their valuable time together to come up with solutions that can change and save lives. It should never be treated casually. So do not put any Tom, Dick or Harry to organize the meeting. Also do not put any Omar, Hassan or Khadijah to organize it either. We must make sure that the person we assign to organize a meeting really knows how to do the job. Let me spell it out further. We must make sure that this person has read this book. There. I have said it. Now let us get back to the Meeting Organizer.

This person can be someone who is not actually participating in the meeting itself or they can be the Chairperson or another attendee to the meeting. The Meeting Organizer has the key responsibility to ensure that all the factors that will contribute to a successful meeting are present.

The success of the actual meeting will of course depend on the Chairperson and attendees themselves. The Meeting Organizer tries to ensure that they have the best chance to succeed.

The Meeting Organizer's role can be divided into three parts: the preparations prior to the meeting, the issues during the meeting and the follow up after the meeting. Let us examine each of these one by one.

The arrangements prior to the meeting are as follows:

- To set an appropriate time, duration and date for the meeting.

- To secure a suitable venue for the meeting (we will detail what a suitable venue is later).

- To coordinate with all relevant parties in the preparation of the agenda (this too will be discussed in detail later).

- To invite, in ample time, the various attendees of the meeting.

- To ensure all items that are needed for the meeting are available such as a coffee maker, overhead projector, white board, etc.

- To get early feedback from those invited to the meeting with regards as to whether they will be attending.

- To plan for the after meeting follow up.

The arrangements during the meeting are as follows:

- If the Meeting Organizer is not physically present during the meeting, they must set up a system that allows the Chairperson to contact them in case of any unexpected emergencies.

- If the Meeting Organizer is on site, then they should ensure that all the arrangements are in place and ready. This can be items such as ensuring the air conditioning is on, the bathrooms are cleaned and the chairs are enough. During the meeting, the Meeting Organizer must also be prepared for unexpected situations such as someone getting sick or the microphone malfunctioning (a very common problem with Islaamic meetings). The Meeting Organizer must be able to anticipate all such problems and be ready to deal with them effectively.

The arrangements after the meeting are as follows:

- The Meeting Organizer should coordinate with the Chairperson to see if there are any pending issues that have to be followed up.

- The Meeting Organizer should execute the after meeting plan such as returning any borrowed items, cleaning up the venue after the meeting, etc.

These are the main roles of the Meeting Organizer. They have the crucial role of ensuring all the external factors regarding the meeting are taken care of. The Chairperson and the attendees are responsible for the internal factors of the meeting (which we shall get to shortly).

20

The Venue

The word venue is used here to mean the place where the meeting will take place. Of course the type and sophistication of the venue will depend on the type of meeting that is to take place. Selecting the right venue for a meeting can be very challenging. However it is actually a skill which can be learned with a bit of practice.

The venue is really an important aspect that contributes to the success of the meeting both physically and psychologically. On a physical level, the security and location of the venue can have a significant impact. On a psychological level, holding a meeting in a fancy place gives the attendees a sense that both the meeting and the attendees are important. This makes them have a positive attitude at the meeting (please, my dear reader, do not give me any lecture about why I should not say "fancy place" as if I am haughty and do not appreciate poor people and scarce resources). So the venue contributes greatly to the success of the meeting. It must be given adequate attention by those who plan meetings. Here are some general guidelines that we must consider when trying to find a venue.

Size

- By this we mean the place where the meeting itself is to be held. Care must be taken to ensure that there is a comfortable space with adequate seating for each person invited to the meeting.

Neighborhood

- We must always be sensitive to the fears and concerns of those who we invite to meetings. The neighborhood of the venue is an important factor as it can affect whether the attendees will want to come or not. If the neighborhood is difficult to reach, or if it is unsafe, or if it does not have parking or such facilities, then the attendees may be reluctant or unwilling to attend.

Location in relation to attendees

- We must always have a keen awareness of where our attendees live and try to pick a location that is fairly central and easy for each of them to reach.

Safety

- This will always be an important factor. We have to ensure that the place where the meeting is to be held is safe for the attendees. None of us want to attend meetings where we feel physically unsafe or we fear for our cars. No matter how committed one is to Islaamic work, it becomes really difficult to attend a meeting if we have to dodge and hide so that we aren't physically assaulted, mugged or attacked. This is not acceptable and it will be difficult to concentrate in the meeting with a busted face or a stolen windshield.

Comfort

- We must try very hard to provide as comfortable a facility as possible for the attendees. After all these attendees are the people who have committed their lives to share the Islaamic lifestyle with others. They make tremendous sacrifices at every step. Thus, the Meeting Organizer should focus on every detail that can provide comfort to the attendees within a particular venue. This involves comfort of the room, air circulation, the comfort of the chairs, the lighting, etc. Other amenities which may enhance the comfort of the meeting include water, electricity, microphone, air condition, overhead projector, whiteboard, bathroom etc. It should be noted that comfort also includes parking facilities which should be safe and adequate.

Price to acquire

- The cost of using or renting a venue is always a factor. This has to be balanced based on the affordability of the group or committee, the importance of the meeting, and the need to convince the attendees to attend the meeting. Generally, it is important to strike a balance here. Do not use a cheap place with poor facilities as this can affect the attendees dramatically from making a meaningful contribution to the meeting.

Duration of use

- It is always important to know exactly how long the venue is to be utilized. This is critical when a price is being paid for the venue. Always leave enough time to cater for any emergencies that may cause the meeting to end later than expected.

Layout of meeting area

- Depending on the meeting type, the layout of the chairs and tables may change. A horse shoe shape layout allows everyone to see each other. However, there are other layouts which should be considered such as the circle layout or the rows layout. The horse shoe layout provides a sense of intimacy with the conductor being at the head. It also makes it possible for the most important attendees to be closer to the conductor. The circle arrangement allows each person to feel an equal sense of importance. All members can see each other. Unfortunately if there are a lot of people the circle can become very wide and the participants may be far apart from each other. The rows layout is similar to a classroom setting. This arrangement causes all the participants to look to the conductor and generally makes it difficult for participants to see or interact with each other. Some thought should be made to ensure that the layout of chairs and tables contribute to the success of the meeting.

Privacy

- Attendees to meeting must be given privacy. It is very difficult to have a meeting that is constantly being interrupted by people who are not part of the meeting. It is even worse to see strangers just come and sit in the meeting even though they have not been invited. The other issue here is that there must be some sense of confidentiality to the meeting. Attendees must be able to speak freely without having their points being quoted or misquoted by every Zaid, Harry or Zainab. Without this privacy the attendees may be reluctant to speak freely or contribute to the meeting.

These are some of the main considerations that must be accounted for when organizing a meeting. As you can see the choice of venue is very important to having a successful meeting. I am fully aware that quite often we may have to meet in a corner of the Masjid or Islaamic center. Sometimes we may not have a choice about catering for any of the above. However, the items mentioned above are meant to give you an idea of what we must strive for. Analysis must be made if the Masjid corner is really producing the quality of meetings we want or not. Is the noise level too great that it disturbs the meeting? Once we recognize that the venue is bad for a meeting, we must work very hard to find a better one.

21

The Agenda

We have now arrived at a very important part of this little book - the Agenda. Wow!

If I had a penny for every bad agenda that crossed my path, I would have been able to make hajj several times already. It is really the place where we commit a major faux pas (I just thought I would use a little French here to impress you. This is pronounced as "foe pa" and it means "a false step." It is when we do something out of the accepted norm). Yes, we butcher the agenda and think that just stringing together a bunch of topics is an agenda. Not so my friend, not so. A well crafted agenda is a masterpiece and a thing of beauty. It is a critical step for the success of the meeting.

Let us first look at some general points regarding the meeting agenda.

- All meetings must have an agenda that is prepared prior to the meeting. It is the agenda that gives birth to the meeting. We must never do it the other way round i.e. to decide to have a meeting and then plan an agenda for it. The need to solve the issues on the agenda is what should trigger the need for the meeting.

- The agenda can be prepared by either the Meeting Organizer, the head of a committee or group or The Chairperson. It all depends on the situation. What is important is that some Shuraa (Islaamic method of consultation) should be done to ensure that relevant persons are able to include what they would like in the agenda.

- The agenda should be distributed as early as possible and certainly before the meeting itself. The methods used to circulate the agenda can be in any manner. It can be phone, email, snail mail, faxes, or whatever other means that makes sense. It should be sent to all those who will be attending the meeting. This is an important step but an overlooked one.

- The agenda should be considered confidential and available only to the members of a particular committee.

It should not be circulated to others who are not in that committee without permission from the Meeting Organizer.

- The agenda must articulate clearly what is to be discussed and decided upon at the meeting. For example instead of saying "picnic", the agenda could say "to identify a suitable venue for the picnic." This allows those attending the meeting to perhaps check out possible venues before coming to the meeting.

- The Meeting Organizer should try to solicit an acknowledgment from those who receive the agenda.

- Generally, the previous minutes should be given to meeting members prior to the current meeting. When this is done the need to re-read the whole minutes verbatim is no longer necessary. Thus in this case the agenda can omit the item of reading of minutes and put instead correction and adoption of minutes.

- Often it is useful to include on the agenda an item called "summary of decisions taken." This is to recap all the decisions taken during the meeting. This is useful in a situation when we are training a young group about meetings or if the meeting is technical and the exact wording of the decisions are vital and critical. This summary should be done preferably by the person who is taking the minutes of the meeting.

- There are two ways of following up assignments and tasks etc. in the minutes. Firstly, if attendees were given copies of the minutes prior to the meeting, they can request that the follow up be a part of the agenda itself. For example, if someone had to check out a venue for a picnic event. The agenda will deal with this pending issue under the agenda item called "picnic follow up." This way is easier to computerize and track. Secondly if the minutes were not circulated to the attendees prior to the meeting, then the follow up items can be addressed as part of the reading, correction and follow up of the minutes itself.

- We should avoid the habit of putting "AOB". This acronym stands for "any other business." Once you allow this to be placed on the agenda especially at the end of the agenda, you are guaranteeing yourself to never finish any meeting on time. This "AOB" works like this. When this item comes up, we turn to the meeting attendees and ask "we will now open the floor for anyone who would like to bring up any other business for discussion." That is when the flood gates open and one or many matters can suddenly appear. The Chairperson is now left to decide if they should put this on the next agenda or deal with it there. It is a bad practice and should not be allowed to happen. A system should be set up so that members are able to have some input regarding the agenda prior to meetings. This ensures that all critical issues will be listed on the agenda and proper time allocated to discuss those issues.

These are some general points concerning the agenda. Now let us look at what must be included in the agenda itself. This is the meat of the matter. This is the real deal.

- The Name of the Committee or Group.

- Meeting Reference Number. This is to identify each meeting.

- The date and time of the meeting.

- The length of the time the meeting is expected to last.

- The venue of the meeting.

- The invitees to the meeting (this is important as members should be aware if some special guest will be there).

- The Chairperson of the meeting (this is because the head may give chairing of certain meetings to others for training purposes).

- The topics for discussion and decision. As mentioned before, the topics should be written in a form that specifies what is to be decided about each topic. (See sample agenda below). If there is additional documentation or information that members require to make a decision, these should be included when the agenda is circulated.

- Approximate time limit for each topic. Be careful with this one. This requires both skill and experience. The Chairperson should try to make this suggested time schedule become a reality.

- Any special remarks. This is to include any other information the expected attendees should know such as whether there is a charge for parking etc.

When your agenda has these items organized in a tasteful and elegant manner, it will give the expected attendees a good feeling about the meeting and it will allow them to think about the items in a clear manner. Thus when the meeting itself takes place, they can quickly give their "pre-thought-out opinions" on each topic. This cuts down on the meeting time.

Well, I hope you are still here with me. Let us look at a sample agenda.

Dear Ashy,

Assalamu 'Alaikum Wa Rahmatullah,

Here is the agenda for the meeting we talked about earlier.

AGENDA:

Committee Name: Picnic Committee

Meeting Ref #   : 53-10052009

Date   : May 10, 2009

Time Duration   : 10:00 A.M. – 11:30 A.M.

Venue   : Broward Library, Room 6, Hollywood Branch

Chairperson   : Sister Alu Kamruz

Invitees   : Sister Kandu, Sister Manila, Sister Hazrah,

                   Sister Ashy

Agenda Items:

1. Correction and Adoption of the past minutes. (5 mins)

2. Picnic: To decide on the best venue (10 mins)

3. Classes: To brainstorm ideas for the new program and assign one person to make a final draft. (30 mins)

4. Progress Reports: To allow members who have previous assignments pending to give a progress report. These are

as follows: Sister Kandu: Library Project; Sister Manila: Feed the poor program. (30 mins)

5. Summary: Reading a summary of the decisions taken at this meeting. (5 mins)

6. Suggestions: Allowing members to suggest items for inclusion at the next meeting. (10 mins)

7. Special Remarks: Please remember to walk with your umbrellas as it may be raining that day. Also lunch will be served.

Special Points on the Above Agenda

The agenda above has an item called progress reports. This should only be used for reports that necessitate further decisions such as a report that says "we report that we have found two venues available." This is useful for the meeting and we can then make a decision of which one is better to use.

Progress reports that do not necessitate a new decision should be sent to the committee members via email by the relevant parties. Valuable meeting time should not be used for distribution or reading of these reports. An example is as follows: "We report that our team had a meeting and we are still checking all possible venues available."

Finally, with regards to the Agenda let me say that the above is just a rough guide. There is no best way to set up the agenda. The key elements that enhance and facilitates the meeting are what we are striving to include in the agenda. I will feel justly rewarded if you will keep these points in mind when planning your next meeting. If you follow some or all of them, it will certainly allow your meetings to be both meaningful and shorter.

Let us re-iterate that each item of the agenda should be worded in such a manner that the attendees know exactly what it is they are expected to make decisions on. Of course most decisions become worthwhile and useful when they are clearly worded and have a person or team and deadline attached to them!

22

The Attendees

No one really wants to spend their time in meetings if given a choice in the matter. Generally, we tend to love meetings that are meaningful and organized and we hate meetings that waste our time and insult our intelligence. The reality is that throughout our lives we will be attending meetings all the time. It is important to learn how to be a good meeting participant.

If we are going to be in meetings it makes good sense to learn how to make them an enjoyable and rewarding experience. I think very few people will disagree with that.

Let us consider some general guidelines for being a good meeting participant.

- Before you leave home it is a good idea to make sure that you brush your teeth and use a suitable mouthwash as you will be close up to other people.

- Dress in an appropriate manner as this will cause others to respect you. After all you are attending a meeting to discuss Islaam and Muslims.

- Use any appropriate perfume if you are a male.

- Always try to be well prepared before coming to a meeting. If you were paying attention to all that I have been saying earlier, you would realize that you should not be attending meetings without being given an agenda prior to it. Once you have the agenda, you can really prepare well.

- As a conscious Muslim you have no choice but to attend the meeting on time. What you can do is not to arrive too early. If for some reason, you are late or cannot make the meeting at all, inform the relevant parties early of your situation. This can be the Meeting Organizer or the Chairperson. If you know of your expected absence early, then try to submit your assignments prior to the meeting.

Also make an effort to find out what took place at the meeting.

- Always find out what is the protocol for the meeting. Different types of meetings have different protocols. For example, ask if you have to put your hands up and get acknowledgment or permission from the Chairperson before you make your point or do you just start talking.

- Always try to present your points in a clear and concise manner. If you did your homework prior to the meeting, this should not be a problem.

- Always show respect for the Chairperson and listen to their instructions and follow them. They have a difficult job and your role is to make it easy for them.

- A meeting is a clash of ideas and opinions. Quite often attendees will be at odds with each other. The advice of Imaam Shafi' is relevant here. He advised that we must put forward our arguments and points with the full conviction that it is the best and most correct one. However we must also leave room for the small possibility that it may be wrong. And in relation to the others, we must argue against them with the full conviction that their arguments are wrong but leave space for the small possibility that they may be right. Thus we must be able to constantly assess what is the best benefit for the entire group and be willing to compromise our opinions and ideas for this purpose.

- It is part of the etiquette of the meeting that in the period of discussion all attendees may vociferously advocate their views and argue passionately in support of them. However, once a group decision is taken, everyone must abide by it and execute it as if it was their own. They are free to personally continue to feel it was a mistake and hold on to their personal views but they must not allow this to negatively affect the execution of the group's decision. As they continue to privately hold on to their personal opinions, they must simultaneously advocate for the group's decisions with the same passion as they did for their own opinion.

- As a Muslim, always show class and speak with respect and decorum. Never lose your cool or get angry. I know in some meetings it is just not practical to do this but every effort must be made to maintain your composure.

- Be very careful to distinguish the issue from the person. We are not allowed to indulge in name calling/slandering and such practices. Keep away from criticizing the person. Focus on their arguments and issues and deal with those alone.

- Develop the character to be recognized as one who is always professional and courteous.

- A sickness I see often in meetings is this attitude of not taking on tasks and responsibilities. Why are we there if it is not to collectively share the burdens and workload? How do we expect to succeed otherwise? As part of a meeting you must recognize that there are consequences and responsibilities that are obligated upon you. Make sure you take on your fair share of the various tasks and assignments or else find another meeting or group that suits your style and demeanor. There, I said it. I know it is harsh but too much is at stake.

- In the delivery and presentation of your assignments show some class and professionalism. Make and distribute copies to the attendees of any report that you have prepared for the meeting.

- During the meeting, be alert and proactive. Concentrate and participate. This is the work of Allah and the decisions taken, no matter how trivial, will affect the lives of others. Do not slouch, giggle, or behave in an unprofessional manner.

- Always make a note for yourself of the assignments that are given to you. Do not wait for the meeting minutes as these may have mistakes and may not be distributed in a timely manner.

- I have emphasized to you that our goal should be to improve the quality of meetings for all. In order to accomplish this, we must always be on the lookout for the common mistakes that occur in meetings and point them out (privately or publicly) to those concerned. This hopefully will give them an opportunity to avoid such mistakes in the future. You can also get them a copy of this book. ☺

- If you take assignments and cannot fulfill them for whatever reasons, please inform the relevant authority as early as possible.

I believe if you follow these guidelines, meetings will become a truly rewarding and beneficial experience for you. You will actually grow as a person and be able to make a huge difference in whatever environment you find yourself in.

23

The Chairperson

You go to bed at night and then wake up screaming loudly. What happened with you last night, your family asks? You look at them in shock and blurt out "I dreamt I was the Chairperson of a meeting."

One of the most difficult jobs is to be a Chairperson. This word used to be Chairman but it is no longer politically correct to say this. It is disrespectful to women. Thus we end up with this strange word "chairperson." This poor soul really has a very difficult job. It is indeed a real challenge to gather brilliant souls and produce from their interaction, a cohesive set of action oriented decisions that they are willing to bring to fruition. Doing this is no small feat. I admire those who do this job. Now if your situation changes and Allah decides to test you and task you with the title Chairperson, listen up.

Here is what you need to be aware of:

- You are responsible for ensuring the agenda is successfully completed.

- You are responsible to facilitate and guide the opinions and discussions of the members of the meeting and not to just impose your personal views and opinions on the discussions.

- You must try to manage the meeting so that no one person is allowed to monopolize the discussion. You should not allow members to engage in intangible discussions.

- As the Chairperson you are also allowed to voice your opinion just like any other member without any extra privilege. The role can be synonymous to that of a captain of a sports team. The captain is a member of the team and must make effort to play as hard as possible, while at the same time ensure that all other team members are being given a chance to play their role as well.

- You have to try to control the discussion by keeping track of the time, summarizing points at the appropriate time, and advocating for a decision. The final decision must be made clear to all so that no member is left unsure or uncertain of it.

- If you are also the head of the group in addition to being the Chairperson, which is pretty common, then you may have certain veto powers that you may invoke based on your organization's bylaws. For example, some groups may not allow a veto if two thirds of the members agree on an issue, etc. Be careful how you do this and use it only in rare situations. It is the fastest way to become unpopular and alienated from the others. It is always better to find ways to get the majority of attendees to agree to the decision.

- You must try to ensure that all members are treated fairly and have enough time to advocate their point of view without disrespect. There will always be opinions that are contrary to yours but you must respect their right to say it.

- In meetings there will be shy persons and it is your job to keep the bullies away from them and make it easy for them to participate in the meeting. Give them a chance to say what they feel.

I want to stop here as most of the skills of the Chairperson really come with experience in dealing with different types of people in different situations. Hopefully with practice we can all learn how to become excellent Chairpersons.

24

The Minutes

Once the meeting is over, the person assigned to document the meeting will send us a copy of the minutes (we hope). The term "minutes" is used to refer to the document that captures all the relevant decisions, suggestions and data for the meeting. It is the legal and official record of the meeting and must be treated with respect and care. It should be confidential to the members of the meeting and should not be circulated to any and everyone without proper permission. Here are some guidelines regarding this document.

- Minutes are to be done by a suitably qualified person.

- A copy of the meeting's minutes must be circulated to all invitees (listed on the agenda) of the meeting.

- Minutes should be circulated by the third day following the meeting or whatever protocol that is established. It is important to establish some protocol to ensure that attendees know when they will receive their minutes and thus can plan the smooth execution of their assignments.

- The minutes of a meeting must be corrected and adopted at the beginning of the next meeting. As mentioned before, since everyone has a copy of the minutes prior to the meeting, it is not necessary to read the whole minutes in the meeting itself.

- One method of adoption of the minutes can be as follows: one member adopts the minutes, and another member will second the adoption (this is optional in some cases). This makes the minutes legal. The official minutes should be signed by the person who prepared it.

- Once the minutes have been adopted by the committee, it should not be changed.

- All minutes of meetings must be carefully catalogued, filed and kept secure.

Remember the minutes of a meeting are just a guideline as there are no specific rules about how to prepare the actual minutes. The key is to remember the minutes should be written in a manner that makes it easy to find the various decisions that were taken. Some groups actually use a color coded system where decisions are in one color and suggestions are in another.

Here are some of the main recommended items that should be in the minutes. Many of these items can be left out based on how formal or informal we want the meeting to be. The best way is to develop a standard form that can be filled in. This gives consistency and makes it easy to capture the relevant information.

- Name of organization (optional)

- Name of Committee

- Reference Number of Minutes

- Venue

- Date

- Duration for each agenda item as well as the whole meeting

- Agenda items

- Chairperson

- Those who attended

- Those who were absent

- Those who were late

- Corrections and additions to the previous minutes

- Who adopted and seconded the last minutes

- Decisions

- Main Suggestions

- Other Important points (this may include ideas or agreements for next meeting's agenda)

Let us take a look at a simple sample Minutes:

Minutes of the Social Committee # C123

The members met on Monday the 12th of October, 2009 at Rich Hall with all members being present and on time. The meeting started on time. The Chairperson for this meeting was Pu. The minutes of the previous meeting was corrected and adopted by Iz and Obur.

Decisions Made:

1.   Salim will visit Davie Park and finalize arrangements for the picnic by Tuesday, Oct 13th, 2009

2.   All members will come out to the bazaar next Friday at 5:00 p.m.

Key Suggestions:

There was one suggestion to change the venue of the meeting to Sammy's Hideout.

Special Remarks:

Remember to walk with your club jacket to the next meeting.

25

Some Suggested Protocols

Meetings represent a forum where humans gather to discuss ideas and make decisions. Quite often when this happens, rituals develop along with procedures. Here are some that are relevant to us.

- It is optional to begin the meeting with a dua' (supplication). This can be the collective recitation of Sura Fatiha or some other dua'.

- Stop the meeting if the Salaah time comes and then after making the Salaah, resume the meeting.

- It is a good idea to have some refreshments at the meeting.

- It is also a good idea to have some paper and pens available for those who may need it.

- Always start the meeting on time as long as the Chairperson, secretary (or the one in charge of the minutes) and two other persons are present. If we do this consistently we will see a wonderful thing happen before our very eyes. No one will come late.

- Those who come late should serve the others during refreshment time and pack up after the meeting.

- Always make it a point to allow late comers to explain why they were late. Do not let them just come to the meeting and sit down quietly as if nothing has happened. Let them know you were concerned about them and ask them what it was that delayed them. This exercise will cause them to feel uncomfortable and hopefully give them the motivation to be early in future meetings.

- Attendees of a meeting do not have to always say "Assalaamu 'Alaikum" when they begin to speak or make a point.

- Give Salaams to the Prophet Muhammad (peace be upon him) when his name is mentioned and encourage the others to do likewise. We should say "peace be upon him" or "sallal laawho 'alaihi wa sallam". We should also say "radiyallaaho anh" (male) or radiyallaaho anhaa (female) for the companions of the Prophet (PBUH). This means "May Allah be pleased with him or her."

- It is always good to remind the Attendees of the meeting that the affairs of the meeting are confidential. Quite often we may quote some person or analyze the behavior of a group or someone during the course of the meeting. Attendees should be discreet and not just go and tell the particular group or person what transpired without permission. This is violating a trust and can result in much hurt and undermining of the success of the meeting itself. It can also lead to severe relationship fractures that may be difficult to mend. Attendees should respect this protocol as it is very important.

- If the meeting members consist of both Muslims and non-Muslims, then care should be taken to make the non-Muslims feel comfortable. This book is too small to go into all these kind of details. For example, explain any Arabic terms that is being used etc.

- On closing the meeting, it is recommended to recite the following dua'. It should be recited collectively so that all members of the meeting can memorize it.

Subhaanaka Allahumma wa bihamdik

Glory be to you, O Lord and with your Praise

Nash hadu an laa ilaaha il laa ant

We testify that there is no God except You.

Nastagfiruka wa na toobu ilaik

We seek Your forgiveness and turn to You in repentance.

- Always end the meeting with Sura 'Asr which is as follows:

Wal 'Asr

By time through the ages

Innal insaana lafee khusr

Mankind is in loss

Illal lazheena aamanoo

except those who believe

wa 'amilus Saalihaat

and do righteous actions

Watawaa sou bil haq

and mutually encourage each other to truth

Watawaa sou bis sabr

and mutually encourage each other to patience

- The practice of embracing each other before departure is a cultural issue and is left to the particular situation.

Members leaving the meeting should always make an effort to forgive each other for any harsh words said at the meeting. The departure should, as a matter of policy, always be a pleasant affair with well wishes to each other and even phrases such as "ma 'asalaama" may the peace be with you or in simple English – go in peace.

26

Summary of Main Ideas

When Invited to a Meeting:

1. Do I need to be physically present?

2. Can you send your input via email or some other manner?

3. Can you come just for the part of the meeting that is relevant to you?

4. If you decide to go then ask for the following:

    a. An agenda

    b. Address of venue and directions

    c. Who else is coming?

    d. How long is the meeting?

    e. Will it start on time?

Examples of problem situations in meetings:

1. Late Start
2. Bored Members
3. Mystery Agenda
4. Digression vs Discussion
5. Missing Data
6. Never Ending Meeting
7. Bullying for Attention
8. Decisions or Pious Wishes
9. Bad Chairperson
10. Poor Venue

Why are Meetings Important:

1. Interaction and sharing of ideas
2. Align perspectives to arrive at an agreed solution
3. Distribution of tasks
4. Make Decisions
5. Solicit suggestions
6. Make friends and network
7. Forum to organize and be organized
8. Force thinking and planning

Role of the Meeting Organizer:

1. Before Meeting:

    a. Set time, duration and date

    b. Secure venue

    c. Prepare agenda

    d. Invite meeting attendees and get feedback

    e. Provide meeting items

    f. Plan follow up

2. During Meeting

    a. If the meeting organizer will not be present, they need to coordinate with the Chairperson

    b. If the meeting organizer is present at the meeting, they must ensure smooth execution

    c. Anticipate any potential problems and be prepared to deal with them

3. After Meeting

    a. Follow up pending issues

    b. Return borrowed items

    c. Organize clean up, etc

Factors to consider when choosing a Venue:

1. Size \ Space

2. Neighborhood

3. Location in relation to attendees

4. Safety

5. Comfort

6. Price to acquire

7. Duration of use

8. Layout of meeting area

9. Privacy

Agenda Issues:

1. All meetings must have an agenda

2. Circulate prior to meeting as early as possible and solicit acknowledgement

3. Prepared by meeting organizer or suitable qualified person

4. Agenda is confidential to those at the meeting

5. Agenda must define what is to be decided upon

6. Do not put reading of minutes in agenda if this is already circulated

7. Include summary of decisions when useful

8. Follow up of past items can be discussed as an agenda item or follow up from the minutes

9. Do not put AOB in the agenda

Items to include in Agenda

1. The Name of the Committee or Group

2. Meeting Reference Number

3. The date and time of the meeting

4. The length of the time the meeting is expected to last

5. The venue of the meeting

6. The invitees to the meeting

7. The Chairperson of the meeting

8. The topics for discussion and decision

9. Approximate time limit for each topic

10. Any special remarks

Guidelines for those attending meetings:

1. Brush your teeth

2. Take a pad and pen

3. Walk with your snacks

4. Leave in time to be punctual

5. Dress appropriately

6. Walk with agenda and previous minutes

7. Have a contact name in case of problems e.g. can't find venue

8. Study agenda and prepare your ideas

9. Ask about meeting protocol

10. Make your points in a clear and concise manner

11. Respect the Chairperson

12. Listen for any instructions

13. Share your points and be willing to listen to others as well

14. Abide by the decisions of the meeting

15. Never lose your cool

16. Be very careful to distinguish the issue from the person

17. Be professional and courteous

18. Be willing to take on assignments and write them down

19. Participate fully

The Chairperson's Role:

1. Ensure agenda is successfully completed

2. Guide discussions

3. Allow all to participate

4. Give your views

5. Monitor time for discussions

6. Be fair to all and show respect

Guidelines for the Minutes:

1. Minutes prepared by qualified person

2. Give each member of meeting a copy at least three days after meeting

3. Correct and adopt minutes at the start of the meeting

4. Do not change the minutes after it is adopted

5. File in secure place

Items to include in the Minutes:

1. Name of organization (optional)

2. Name of Committee

3. Reference Number of Minutes

4. Venue

5. Date

6. Duration for each agenda item

7. Agenda items

8. Chairperson

9. Those who attended

10. Those who were absent

11. Those who were late

12. Corrections and additions to the previous minutes

13. Who adopted and seconded the last minutes

14. Decisions

15. Main Suggestions

16. Other Important points

Some Meeting Protocols:

1. Optional starting dua'

2. Stop the meeting for Salaah

3. Provide refreshments

4. Provide paper and pens

5. Start on time if Chairperson, secretary and two other persons are present.

6. Latecomers serve and clean up

7. Solicit excuses from late comers

8. No need to give salaams every time before making your point

9. Send salutation to the Prophet (SA) and Sahabahs (RA)

10. Meetings are confidential to meeting members

11. Explain Arabic terms

12. Make dua' to close meeting

13. Recite Sura 'Asr before departure

14. Meet meeting members and leave amicably

27

Thanks For Taking A Chance

If you are still here after all that I have just put you through then you are indeed special. I want to commend and congratulate you. It tells me that you are serious about this mission of getting rid of bad meetings. I wish you well and thank you for making this journey with me! May Allah bless you to become an advocate for this noble cause!

I hope you found this little book beneficial and useful. If in some way I have helped you to become a better meeting planner or attendee, then my goal was accomplished. Please help this effort which is done solely for the "pleasure of Allah." If you would like to sponsor future projects, then please contact us. We hope to also produce literature on teaching, program planning, conducting study circles, etc

May Allah reward you and your family with goodness in this world and in the next as well and make your final meeting with Him successful!

Ameen!

www.ingramcontent.com/pod-product-compliance
Lightning Source LLC
Chambersburg PA
CBHW022106210326
41520CB00045B/426